W9-BLY-190

Cool ROCKS

Creating Fun *and* Fascinating Collections!

Tracy Kompelien

ABDO
Publishing Company

Visit us at
www.abdopublishing.com

Published by ABDO Publishing Company, 4940 Viking Drive, Edina, Minnesota 55435.
Copyright © 2007 by Abdo Consulting Group, Inc. International copyrights reserved in all countries.
No part of this book may be reproduced in any form without written permission from the publisher.
The Checkerboard Library™ is a trademark and logo of ABDO Publishing Company.

Printed in the United States.

Design and Production: Mighty Media, Inc.
Cover Photo: Anders Hanson
Interior Photos: Anders Hanson; Shutterstock; The following manufacturers/names appearing in
Cool Rocks are trademarks: Sharpie® (p. 26), Kids Choice Glue® (pp. 26, 29)
Series Editor: Pam Price

Library of Congress Cataloging-in-Publication Data

Kompelien, Tracy, 1975-
  Cool rocks / Tracy Kompelien.
     p. cm. -- (Cool collections)
  Includes index.
  ISBN-13: 978-1-59679-771-0
  ISBN-10: 1-59679-771-1
 1. Rocks--Collection and preservation. 2. Rocks--Study and teaching--Activity programs. 3. Petrology
I. Title. II. Series: Cool collections (Edina, Minn.)

QE433.6.K66 2007
552.075--dc22

                                                        2006011965

Contents

This Planet Rocks!

DID YOU KNOW THAT THE EARTH IS MADE MOSTLY OF ROCKS? Rocks are everywhere on the earth! Rocks are in oceans and lakes. They're underground and above ground. They come in all shapes and sizes. They can be as big as a mountain or as small as a piece of sand.

Geologists are scientists who study the earth. They have been able to learn a lot about the earth's history by studying all types of ancient rocks. Some of these rocks are millions of years old.

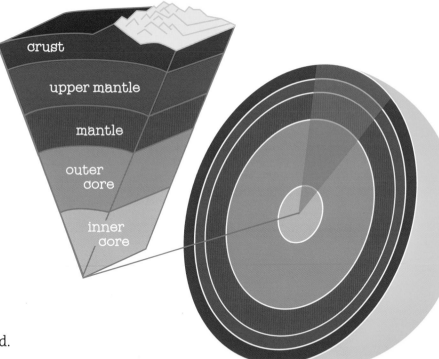

crust

upper mantle

mantle

outer core

inner core

Most rocks on the surface of the earth are a combination of up to eight elements. These are oxygen, silicon, aluminum, iron, calcium, sodium, potassium, and magnesium. These elements make up most of the weight of the earth's crust.

Common Rock Elements

O
Oxygen

Si
Silicon

Al
Aluminum

Fe
Iron

Ca
Calcium

Na
Sodium

K
Potassium

Mg
Magnesium

Rock Groups

THERE ARE THREE GROUPS OF ROCKS. It is important to understand the **characteristics** of these groups if you want to be a collector. Then you will be able to classify your rocks just as geologists and avid rock collectors do! So what determines which group a rock is part of? It's all in how the rock was formed! Below are some examples of rocks in each group.

Igneous		Sedimentary	Metamorphic
Andesite	Granite	Breccia	Gneiss
Basalt	Obsidian	Conglomerate	Marble
Diabase	Pumice	Dolomite	Quartzite
Diorite	Rhyolite	Limestone	Schist
Gabbro	Scoria	Sandstone	Serpentinite
		Shale	Slate

Obsidian

Scoria

Granite

Basalt

Igneous Rocks

Igneous rocks are the oldest rocks on earth. They are made up of old rocks that have melted together. The temperature deep below the surface of the earth is so high that rocks turn into liquid. The liquid is called magma. When magma cools, igneous rocks are formed.

Sometimes magma seeps into cracks that are underneath the ground and hardens. Other times, volcanoes force magma to the surface of the earth where it cools, hardens, and turns back into a solid igneous rock. No two igneous rocks are the same, because they all cool differently!

Sandstone

Limestone

Shale

Dolomite

Sedimentary Rocks

Sedimentary rocks are made of layers of small bits of plant, animal, rock, or mineral material. If you look closely, you can usually see several layers of color in a sedimentary rock. The different colors are from the different types of sediment that came together to form that rock.

Sedimentary rocks are formed two different ways. Sometimes layers of sediment build up and the lower layers are pressed together by the weight of the upper layers. The pressure causes the sediment to solidify into one rock. Other times, minerals act like glue and hold several sediment layers together.

Metamorphic Rocks

Metamorphic rocks were once sedimentary or igneous rocks. Enormous pressure and heat under the earth's crust changes the structure of existing rocks until they become new types of rocks. This process, called metamorphism, or morphing, is how metamorphic rocks are formed.

So where do the heat and pressure come from? The pressure is from layers of rock that pile up. The more layers there are, the greater the pressure on the bottom rock. The heat comes from magma.

When there is enough heat and pressure, a rock can morph into a different type of rock. For example, limestone can morph into marble, and shale can morph into slate.

Marble

Quartzite

Gneiss

Slate

Stormy Weather

Weather has a big effect on rocks. Wind, water, and ice wear rocks down into small pieces, or sediment. The small pieces are then carried to lakes, rivers, streams, and oceans by water or wind. There they sit at the bottom of the body of water. As the water moves them around, they often get pressed together and harden back into larger rocks. This process usually happens underwater and takes millions of years. So there's no need to worry, your favorite rock won't change shape overnight!

Rock

Mineral

Mineral or Rock?

IT IS IMPORTANT TO KNOW THE DIFFERENCE BETWEEN ROCKS AND MINERALS. Rocks are solid substances that are made up of two or more minerals. For example, granite is made when the minerals quartz, feldspar, and mica come together.

Minerals are nonliving, solid substances found in the earth. They are almost always found in crystal form. And unlike rocks, minerals are always the same shape. So if you found pieces of pyrite in both North America and Europe, they would both have cube-shaped crystals.

Everyday Minerals

Minerals are around us every day. If you put salt on your food, you are putting the mineral halite on it! The toothpaste you brush your teeth with contains an important mineral, fluoride. Your pencil even has the mineral graphite in it!

Fun Facts about Rocks

1 Basalt is the most common rock on earth.

2 Stone Age hunters often made tools and weapons of sharpened pieces of flint.

3 Many of today's lapis lazuli gemstones come from age-old mines in Afghanistan. These same mines supplied the lapis lazuli worn by the pharaohs of ancient Egypt.

4 Mount Rushmore National Memorial features the faces of four U.S. presidents carved in granite.

5 Marble is made mostly of calcium, just like your teeth!

6 Pumice is the only rock that floats in water.

Collection Tools

EVERY ROCK TELLS A STORY ABOUT THE EARTH, WHICH IS JUST ONE OF THE REASONS IT IS SO FUN TO START A ROCK COLLECTION. To start your collection, you must first find the rocks. Before you begin, gather the tools you will need. Here's a list to get you started.

What You Need

- Sandwich bags
- Small shovel or spade
- Permanent marker
- Journal
- Bucket, bag, or backpack to carry your rocks
- Magnifying glass
- Labels

Become a Rock Hound!

A GOOD PLACE TO START LOOKING FOR ROCKS IS RIGHT OUTSIDE YOUR FRONT DOOR. Take a walk. Visit your backyard, a park, the beach, a playground, or a nearby river or lake.

While you look, pay close attention to the texture and color of the rocks you see. You may need to use your shovel or spade to dig for the rocks. As you pick up each rock, put it in a sandwich bag and stick a label on the bag. Write a number on the label to help you sort and identify the rocks later.

June 7, 2006

#1

Take Notes!

Write some notes in your journal about each rock you find. First write down the number from the label. Then write down a few details. Creating a rock chart in your journal is a good way to organize your findings. List the number from the label, the date, and where you found the rock. Make some notes about the rock's size, color, texture, and shape.

Be Responsible

Responsible rock hounds respect other people and they respect the earth.

• Make sure you get permission when hunting rocks on private property!

• Try not to litter roads or sidewalks with your rocks.

• Never throw rocks at people or animals.

• Try to leave your rock collecting area just as you found it.

• Always go with an adult or friend. Be sure to let an adult know where you are going and when you will be back!

On the Go

Rock collecting is a hobby that goes everywhere you do. Wherever you travel, you'll see rocks. Try to notice how they are different from rocks back home. Pick out a few nice samples to add to your collection. But don't pick up too many. Hauling home a suitcase full of rocks can be a real drag!

Cleaning Rocks

ONCE YOU'VE HAULED HOME A BUNCH OF ROCKS, IT'S TIME TO CLEAN THEM UP!

Fill a container with warm, soapy water. Wash each rock one at a time. You may want to use an old toothbrush to help you scrub the rocks clean. Then wipe each rock with a cloth or a paper towel. Set the damp rocks on some newspaper and place each rock's bag next to it. Wait until they are completely dry and then put the rocks back into their bags.

What You Need

- Deep bowl, pot, or bucket full of water
- Mild dish soap
- Old rags or paper towels
- Newspaper (optional)
- Soft toothbrush (optional)

Identifying Rocks

THERE ARE MANY BOOKS THAT CAN HELP YOU IDENTIFY ROCKS AND MINERALS. You can also use this chart to help identify your rocks! Don't worry if you can't **pinpoint** a certain rock right away. You can figure it out later and then add the information to your rock journal.

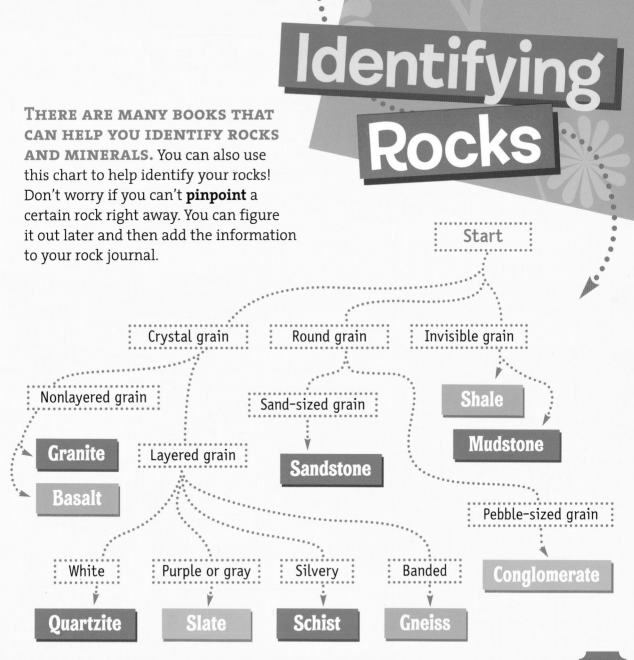

Start

Crystal grain → Round grain → Invisible grain

Nonlayered grain

Sand-sized grain

Shale

Granite

Basalt

Layered grain

Sandstone

Mudstone

Pebble-sized grain

White → Quartzite

Purple or gray → Slate

Silvery → Schist

Banded → Gneiss

Conglomerate

Housing
Your Rocks

AFTER YOU'VE DONE THE HARD WORK OF COLLECTING AND IDENTIFYING YOUR ROCKS, YOU'LL WANT TO ORGANIZE THEM. Old checkbook boxes, shoe boxes, and egg cartons all make good homes for your collection. You also can buy boxes that have compartments. Stick with small boxes though. Otherwise they'll get too heavy when you fill them.

If you can, try to group similar rocks together. Be sure to label the rocks as you put them in the boxes. You can use the labels from the collecting bags or make new ones. You should also label the outside of the boxes. Then you can quickly find what you're looking for later.

18

Rock Solid

As your collection grows, go through your rocks and get rid of any that aren't valuable to you and your collection. Also make a list of any rocks you want but don't have. If there are some rocks you really want but cannot find yourself, consider buying them.

Rock shops are full of beautiful, tempting things. So, it's really easy to get carried away and buy too much! Figure out a budget before you go. You need to know what you want and research what it costs. If there aren't any rock shops in your town, check the Internet. There are many good Web sites to order rocks from. Be sure to ask an adult to help you when ordering rocks online.

Rock and Roll!

POLISHED ROCKS ARE A NICE ADDITION TO ANY ROCK COLLECTION.
Or, you can use them as something functional, such as jewelry or a paperweight. The way to polish a rock is with a rock tumbler. You will need a rock tumbler kit, which can be found at creative science stores, hobby shops, and on the Internet.

Rock tumbling is a process that transforms rough stones into shiny, smooth stones. It can take a long time, sometimes as long as a month! And, it's always good to have a parent or other adult help you.

A rock tumbler works by rotating rocks inside a barrel. The rotation removes all of the rough edges from the rocks. A grinding powder is used first to duplicate the natural erosion process. Then, once the stone has been shaped, another powder is added to polish the rock until it's perfectly smooth.

Tumbled rocks

Untumbled rocks

Tumbling Tips

- Don't tumble hard and soft stones together.
- Gravel and beach stones are good materials to begin with.
- Remember, rock tumblers are very noisy! Put your tumbler someplace in the house where it won't disturb anyone.

Trimming Rocks

MANY ROCK HOUNDS TRIM THE ROCKS THEY FIND.
The goal of trimming a rock is to improve its overall appearance and quality. You want to be able to see the **distinguishing** qualities of the rock.

Hammers for Hounds

A geologist's hammer is a special hammer. It is heavier than most household hammers. One side of the head has a flat surface for hammering. The other side has either a pick or a chisel.

Experienced collectors often break rocks while they're out collecting. They use very heavy hammers to do this. When they get the rock home, they use smaller hammers and chisels to break more pieces off the rock. It takes a lot of knowledge about rocks before you know where to hit them to achieve the results you want.

Some rock hounds trim rocks to remove any unattractive bits. Others just want to make them smaller! It's desirable to have rocks that are about the same size in a collection. A common size is two inches by four inches by three inches.

If you want to try trimming a rock, start by practicing on rocks that you wouldn't normally keep. Always wear safety glasses and have an adult help you.

Breaking a Geode

A GEODE IS FORMED WHEN FLUIDS CRYSTALLIZE INSIDE A ROCK. The exterior is usually limestone. The inside contains quartz crystals or **chalcedony** deposits. Some geodes are completely filled with crystals. These geodes are called nodules.

The size, form, and color of the crystals can vary greatly, making each geode unique. Some are clear quartz crystals. Others have rich purple amethyst crystals. Still others contain agate, chalcedony, or jasper crystals.

You can buy geodes at rock shops, science museums, or online. Of course, you won't really know what you bought until you open the geode. The fun part of geodes is the surprise you get when you open them up! All you need to open a geode is a hammer and a sock and an adult to supervise you.

As Easy As...

1 Put a geode in a sock.

2 Lay the sock on a hard surface, such as a garage floor or a concrete sidewalk.

3 Carefully hammer the geode until it breaks.

Join the Club!

ROCK CLUBS ARE GREAT PLACES TO MEET PEOPLE WHO SHARE YOUR INTEREST IN ROCK COLLECTING! If you want to join a rock club, ask the staff at a rock store or a science museum about local clubs. If they don't know of any local clubs, search the Internet. There might be some local clubs the staff doesn't know about.

If you have trouble finding a rock club, start one yourself! Ask the school or the local community center if you can meet there. Set a date for the first meeting and put up posters around school inviting people to come. Talk to people around you about your new hobby. Some of them might be interested in going on a rock-collecting adventure!

Here are some ideas for something to do at the first meeting of your new club:

• Talk about the different kinds of rocks in your area.

• Ask everyone to bring in a rock to share with the others.

• Take a short "rock walk" to show others what you can find right outside your back door.

On the Agenda

It's important to make club meetings fun, so plan your **agenda** carefully. Consider doing some of the projects in this book, such as rock tumbling and making pet rocks. You can also invite guest speakers. Choose a topic the group wants to learn about. Then ask staff at the science museum or a rock shop if they will come talk about that subject.

Rock Dominoes

MAKE A PERSONALIZED SET OF DOMINOES.
You can keep them for yourself, but they also make a great gift!

Take a walk and find 28 smooth, flat rocks. They should be about three inches long and about an inch wide. After you are done collecting, take the rocks home and wash them. Let them dry completely.

Pick a paint pen and draw a line across each rock. Then add dots on each side of the line. Use every combination of the numbers zero through six. After the paint dries, you are ready to play! Store your dominoes in a nice box or a cloth bag.

What You Need

- 28 flat rocks
- White or colored paint pens
- Nice box or bag

Pet Rocks

DO YOU WANT A PET THAT YOU WON'T HAVE TO TAKE ON WALKS OR FEED?
Then you want a pet rock!

Take a look at the rocks you have collected and think about what animal the shapes remind you of. You can begin by arranging your rocks to see what you come up with. Large rocks work well for the body, while smaller rocks work well for the feet, eyes, and head. Perhaps you will see a lizard, a frog, or a ladybug as you rearrange the rocks.

What You Need

- Paint pens
- Clean rocks
- Glue (cement glue works well)
- Clay
- Craft sticks (optional)

Once your rocks are arranged, you can begin to glue them together. If you use cement glue, make sure you work in a well-ventilated area. It is a good idea to start with the largest rock. You can use clay to hold the rocks in place until the glue dries.

In the meantime, make a sketch of the finished pet rock. Decide what colors you will use and where they will go.

Now it's time to paint! Use paint pens to draw the eyes, fur, spots, or anything else on your new pet.

If the animal you made is wobbly, you can use a craft stick to make it more stable. Just break a stick to the correct length and glue it to the back of the rocks. You can paint the stick to match the rock so it doesn't show.

Rock Messages

ON YOUR NEXT ROCK-COLLECTING ADVENTURE, BE SURE TO GRAB SOME SMOOTH ROCKS. You can turn these into great gifts to give to your family, friends, or teachers.

You Rock!

Write your message on the rock. Consider **inspirational** words such as *love*, *strength*, and *wonder*. Use a marker to write on light-colored rocks. Paint pens work well on dark rocks.

You can jazz up your rock by adding a piece of brightly colored felt. Cut a large heart or star shape out of a piece of felt. Make sure the shape you cut is about two times the size of the rock. Glue the rock to the center of the felt and let it dry. The felt will protect the surface of the desk or table. You now have a rockin' paperweight!

What You Need

- Permanent marker or paint pen
- Felt
- Glue

Rockin' Frame

SMALL PEBBLES ARE EASY TO FIND.
Just take a look in the garden or even in the driveway. Once you have collected a lot of small pebbles, wash and dry them.

Apply a thick coat of glue to part of the frame. Cover only as much of the frame as you think you can cover with rocks before the glue dries.

Quickly arrange the pebbles on the glue. Then sprinkle glitter over the pebbles, if you wish. It will stick to the glue between the pebbles.

Working in small areas, repeat these steps until the frame is finished.

What You Need

- Small pebbles or rocks
- Glitter, glitter beads, or seed beads (optional)
- Picture frame (remove glass)
- Glue
- A picture you want framed!

Rock Bottom

NOW YOU KNOW HOW ROCKS ARE FORMED, WHERE TO FIND THEM, AND HOW TO MAKE THEM LOOK THEIR BEST. You are a full-fledged rock hound! Rock collecting is a lifelong hobby that becomes more interesting every time you go on a hunt. Not only is it fun to hunt for and collect rocks but you can create a wonderful collection to show your friends and classmates.

No collection is ever complete, so always keep your eyes peeled for new rocks. And remember, the most important part of collecting is to have have fun!

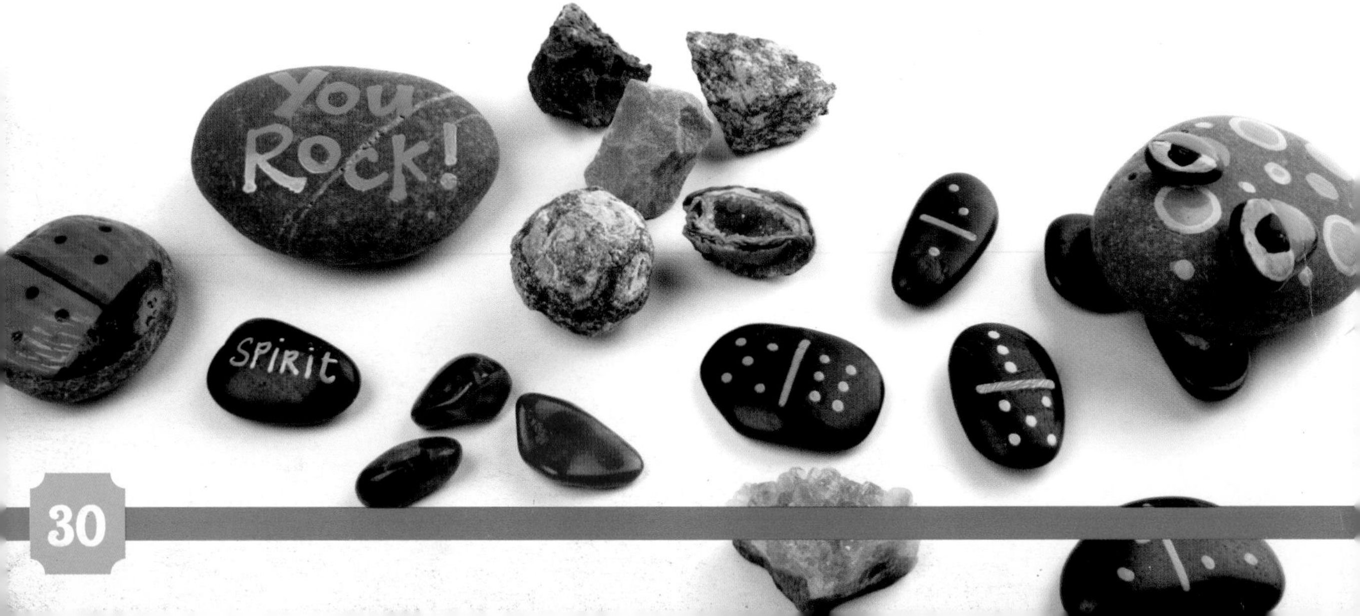
You Rock!
Spirit

Glossary

agenda – a plan or a list of things to do or talk about.

chalcedony – a type of quartz that is milky or grayish and can be semitransparent.

characteristic – a trait or quality that identifies something as different from others in a group.

distinguish – to mark as different from the others.

inspirational – something that motivates or encourages.

pinpoint – to identify accurately.

Web Sites

To learn more about collecting rocks, visit ABDO Publishing on the World Wide Web at **www.abdopublishing.com**. Web sites about rock collecting are featured on our Book Links page. These links are routinely monitored and updated to provide the most current information available.

Index